I0605342

Discovering Norse Mythology

Epic Quests and Adventures OF NORSE MYTHOLOGY

Don Nardo

San Diego, CA

© 2026 ReferencePoint Press, Inc.
Printed in the United States

For more information, contact:
ReferencePoint Press, Inc.
PO Box 27779
San Diego, CA 92198
www.ReferencePointPress.com

ALL RIGHTS RESERVED.
No part of this work covered by the copyright hereon may be reproduced or used in any form or by any means—graphic, electronic, or mechanical, including photocopying, recording, taping, web distribution, or information storage retrieval systems—without the written permission of the publisher.

LIBRARY OF CONGRESS CATALOGING-IN-PUBLICATION DATA

Names: Nardo, Don, 1947- author.
Title: Epic quests and adventures of Norse mythology / by Don Nardo.
Description: San Diego, CA : ReferencePoint Press, Inc., [2025] | Series: Discovering Norse mythology | Includes bibliographical references and index.
Identifiers: LCCN 2024049074 (print) | LCCN 2024049075 (ebook) | ISBN 9781678210328 (library binding) | ISBN 9781678210335 (ebook)
Subjects: LCSH: Mythology, Norse--Juvenile literature.
Classification: LCC BL860 .N255 2025 (print) | LCC BL860 (ebook) | DDC 398.20948--dc23/eng/20241206
LC record available at https://lccn.loc.gov/2024049074
LC ebook record available at https://lccn.loc.gov/2024049075

CONTENTS

An Adventurous People

The fabled Norse hero Sigurd did not embark on his daring quest for vengeance to please himself. Instead, he intended to achieve justice for his foster father and guardian, Regin. One day Regin, a skilled blacksmith and sword maker, took Sigurd, then in his late teens, aside and told him about the disturbing events that had devastated Regin's family several years before. Regin's father, the sorcerer Hreidmar, had managed to amass a vast treasure composed of objects of pure gold. Hreidmar had intended to divide that wealth equally among his sons, but Regin's greedy brother, Fafnir, wanted it all for himself. First, Fafnir slew Hreidmar. Then the young murderer, who was a dwarf with the power to shape-shift, transformed himself into a dragon and took the treasure to a cave in the wilderness. There, the monster guarded the gold day and night.

Fafnir
A dwarf who could transform into a dragon

Hearing about these fateful events, Sigurd was appalled. In historian Daniel McCoy's telling of the tale, Sigurd told Regin, "I'm truly sorry for your loss."[1] He then offered to avenge his guardian's misfortunes by tracking down and killing Fafnir. In preparation for that dangerous quest, the young man first searched for a suitable horse. One day while he was walking through a forest, he saw a handsome gray stallion standing beside a tall, one-eyed man. The stallion's name was Grani, the tall man told Sigurd. And it was descended from Sleipnir, the magnificent steed belonging to Odin, leader of the Norse gods.

For a small sum, the man said, Sigurd could buy Grani, which was so strong it could easily carry two riders. After buying the horse, Sigurd rode it away, not realizing that the one-eyed man was none other than Odin himself.

Sigurd
A young hero who tracked down and killed the dragon Fafnir

When Sigurd returned to Regin's house, the two men gathered some provisions, mounted Grani, and set off toward the rocky wasteland where Fafnir guarded the treasure. Arriving there three days later, Sigurd and Regin discussed a workable strategy for slaying the huge creature. "The best way," Regin suggested, "will be to dig a ditch across his pathway, crouch down in it, and then stab him in the heart when he crawls to his watering hole."[2]

Sigurd wisely took that advice. He dug the ditch and then hid inside it and waited. Sure enough, a few hours later Fafnir exited the cave, and as the enormous animal passed overhead, the young warrior forcefully thrust his sword upward. Mortally wounded, the dragon thrashed back and forth while torrents of blood spurted from the wound in its chest.

Suddenly seeing Sigurd holding the bloody sword, the dying Fafnir told him the treasure was cursed and would cause great grief, or even death, for anyone who owned it. Wise beyond his years, Sigurd calmly replied, "That is true of all wealth. Everyone wants it for himself, until the day when others kill him to take it for themselves. As for you, your hoard already belongs to another, and you already belong to Hel [the Norse goddess of death]."[3] Those were the last words the beast ever heard, as with a massive thud its gargantuan bulk crashed to the ground.

Tales That Uplifted and Entertained

This story of the hero Sigurd's expedition to slay the dragon Fafnir was well known and often retold in villages across northern Europe when the Norse were at the height of their power and influence. Also commonly called the Vikings, the Norse were the robust, resilient, and frequently warlike residents of Scandinavia and Iceland during the mid-medieval period. From shortly before 800 CE to

Origins of Norse Mythology

shortly after 1000 CE, groups of them frequently raided the coasts of England, Ireland, France, and other parts of western Europe.

Not all Vikings were warriors and raiders, however. Many were farmers, fishers, merchants, and craftspeople. Also, their political and social customs and goals varied from one region to another. A cultural trait that virtually all Norse groups shared, however, was a devout belief in a large group of colorful gods and goddesses. And closely connected to those deities was a collection of myths describing both them and several larger-than-life human rulers and heroes.

Among the most famous and most often retold tales in that collection were those involving large-scale adventures. These included quests to find treasure, gain wisdom, and seek justice;

major military or exploratory expeditions; and long, difficult journeys undertaken by gods and humans alike. Modern scholars have debated why the theme of epic adventure so fascinated the Norse. One reason often cited is that the Vikings were an ambitious, adventurous people. As Norway's official online travel guide explains, the medieval Vikings were

> characterized by their courageous, fatalistic outlook which made them naturally born risk takers. The raiding groups seem to have had a fantastic ability to shrug off losses. . . . The number of deaths caused by war was sometimes shockingly high in relation to the total Viking population. But it did not satisfy their hunger for conquest and exploration for around 250 years.[4]

Other experts have proposed that the Norse fascination for large-scale undertakings and adventures was partly a reaction to the often-difficult realities of life in the Viking lands. In this view, dwelling in the generally cold, mountainous wilderness areas of northern Europe was often a challenge. And most Norse were thirsty for any positive diversions from the difficulties of day-to-day survival. The late, great scholar of medieval Scandinavia, H.R.E. Davidson, pointed out that repeating tales describing action-filled quests and adventures was both entertaining and uplifting. Such myths, she wrote, made "a vigorous, heroic comment on life—life as [people] found it in hard and inhospitable lands."[5]

The All-Father's Quests for Wisdom

A tall one-eyed man wearing an ankle-length cloak walked alone down a dirt road near the southern border of Asgard. Home of the Norse gods, the Aesir, that realm covered thousands of square miles and featured several mountain ranges with numerous fertile valleys running through them. A few birds flying overhead were the only beings who noticed when the tall man reached the Iving River. Both wide and deep, it marked the boundary between Asgard and Jotunheim, the realm of the Jotnar, which in the old Norse language meant "giants." Some Jotnar were indeed huge creatures who towered over humans, yet other so-called giants were no bigger than people. One thing that most of the Jotnar had in common, though, was that they disliked, and sometimes even hated, the gods and humans alike.

The tall man found a small rowboat hidden among some reeds on the riverbank and used the craft to reach the opposite shore. After that, he walked for several hours until he reached a large stone castle. Knocking on the front gate, he was greeted by a female giant who was not much taller than himself, and the man introduced himself as Gagnrad. He said he had come to seek an audience with the castle's owner, Vafthrudnir, who had a reputation for being the smartest and friendliest of all the Jotnar.

Vafthrudnir
A giant whom Odin bested in a contest to see who was most knowledgeable

Soon Gagnrad and Vafthrudnir, who was more than three times the visitor's height, faced each other in the giant's dining hall. Gagnrad explained that he had come to engage Vafthrudnir in a contest—a battle of wits to see which one was the most knowledgeable. Grinning, the giant accepted the challenge, and the two began a long question-and-answer session. At one point, Gagnrad said, "Tell me this one thing if your mind is sufficient and you, Vafthrudnir, know from where the earth came." Quick to answer, Vafthrudnir replied that Odin, leader of the Aesir, had killed the first of the giants—Ymir—and from that monstrous being's flesh "earth was shaped." Furthermore, the mountains were fashioned from Ymir's bones, "and the sea from his blood."[6] Other questions concerned the origins of the sun and moon, where the winds came from, and more facts about the structure and history of the world.

Notably, both contestants repeatedly gave the right answers. Finally, after many hours, Gagnrad asked, "What did Odin say into his son's ear?" At this, Vafthrudnir raised his eyebrows. It struck him that only Odin or his son could correctly answer that question, which meant that Gagnrad was likely to be Odin in disguise. "No man knows what you said in bygone days into your son's ear," Vafthrudnir said, producing a smile. Realizing he had been outwitted, the giant admitted defeat and told his guest, "I've been contending with Odin in words of wisdom." The problem, Vafthrudnir added, was that it was well known that Odin had been scouring the world for knowledge for untold numbers of centuries. And no one could best that deity in a contest involving facts and information. "You'll always be the wisest of beings!"[7] Vafthrudnir exclaimed.

Core Concepts of Viking Philosophy

The contest between the giant Vafthrudnir and Odin was not the only example of a journey taken by that god to find or confirm the correctness of knowledge. Indeed, according to the surviving collection of Norse myths, Odin went on several quests to acquire one form of wisdom or another. Today people who are learning about Viking culture and history for the first time are often surprised by those tales. They wonder why it is that medieval warriors famous for raiding and pillaging also engaged in philosophical thought, including the importance of wisdom and social values.

Their prowess as warriors aside, the Norse desired to lead honest, ethical, and satisfying everyday lives. With those goals in mind, the deeper thinkers among them developed moral maxims, or sayings, to help people make good decisions. Sometime between 900 and 1000 CE, many such proverbs were collected into a document known as the *Havamal*, or "Sayings of the High One." Not surprisingly, the High One was thought to be Odin, also frequently called the All-Father. One of the best-known and most influential of these sayings goes: "Cattle die, kinsmen die, one dies oneself in the same way, but a reputation never dies for the one who acquires a good one."[8]

Wisdom was an important value in Norse mythology. Aesir ruler Odin (pictured) went on several quests to acquire knowledge.

wyrd
Personal destiny or fate

Although everyone was expected to strive to create and maintain a good reputation, complicating matters was one of the core concepts of Viking philosophy. It held that in large degree a person's *wyrd*, or destiny, was ordained by either the gods or mysterious forces that decided even the gods' fates. To face destiny with courage and honor was seen as the greatest moral act. And to better understand fate and other universal mysteries, Odin, who was known for his prowess as a warrior, purportedly devoted much of his life to searching for hidden knowledge. As H.R.E. Davidson astutely pointed out, in the Vikings' eyes, Odin possessed the abilities of both a warrior and poet-scholar, a rare and powerful combination.

The All-Father Pays a Heavy Price

A warrior's bravery and a scholar's thirst for knowledge were both on display in one of the All-Father's best-known quests. At that expedition's core was Odin's fervent desire to learn about some of nature's innermost workings. To acquire such secret knowledge, he knew that he would need to seek out and question a highly elusive and mysterious being named Mimir. Sometimes referred to as the god of wisdom, Mimir was said to dwell in a cave situated in a distant expanse of unpopulated wilderness. There he guarded a magical wellspring known as *Mímisbrunnr*, meaning "Mimir's Well." Legends claimed that its dark waters held immense stores of knowledge, including much about nature's mysteries. There were also rumors claiming that Mimir had absorbed that knowledge by drinking from the fabled spring.

It took Odin many days to walk from Asgard to the vast forested wilderness where Mimir's lair lay. The tall traveler found the cave and spring in a picturesque grove of shade trees resting beside a large granite outcrop. Stopping beside the pool, with its still, murky waters, the All-Father glanced toward the cave entrance. There he caught sight of an extremely old being sitting atop a flat rock. It had been close to a century since Odin had seen Mimir, but there was no mistaking the features of the ancient deity who had been collecting wisdom even longer than Odin had. Similarly, Mimir clearly recognized the visitor. "Hail Odin, eldest of the gods,"[9] Mimir murmured, according to the late Irish poet and mythologist Padraic Colum's retelling of the Norse legends.

Odin walked closer and said, "I would drink from your well," to which Mimir retorted, "There is a price to be paid. All who have come here to drink have shrunk from paying that price." When Odin asked what the price was, the other god explained that the visitor would have to cut out his right eye and toss it into the pond. After a brief moment's thought, the All-Father replied, "I will not shrink from the price that has to be paid."[10]

True to his word, with a dramatic flourish Odin pulled a knife from within his cloak. As Mimir watched, unmoving, the visitor swiftly scooped out his eye and thew it into shadowy *Mímisbrunnr*. The pool's guardian then kept his side of the bloody bargain by filling a drinking horn with water from the well and handing it to the now one-eyed god. Only seconds after Odin swallowed the liquid, he detected a powerful inrush of information about the natural world. Meanwhile, Colum wrote, the lost eye sank deep

Tales of Mimir

Mimir, who guards the well of knowledge lying near the entrance to his cave, was one of the more unusual of the Aesir, the Norse gods inhabiting the realm of Asgard. His origins are largely shrouded in mystery. But some small clues in a few medieval writings suggest that he may have been born a giant. Later in life, that story goes, in some unknown way he joined the Aesir and became a key adviser to Odin. More certain is that Mimir was consistently associated with pursuing and accumulating knowledge on a wide array of subjects. And the Norse often referred to him as the deity of wisdom. Although the story in which he demanded one of Odin's eyes is likely Mimir's best-known myth today, he appears in several less-famous tales. In one, he convinced Heimdall, guardian of the rainbow bridge, to exchange an ear for a drink from the magical well. In another myth, the Vanir, a race of fertility gods, cut off Mimir's head and sent it to Odin, who used mystical herbs to preserve it and keep it alive. After that, from time to time the leader of the Aesir asked his old adviser's head for advice.

This image shows a Viking raid. The Vikings were famous for raiding and pillaging; however, wisdom and societal values were also important to them.

into the well. And there it stayed, "shining up through the water, a sign to all who came to that place of the price that the father of the gods had paid for his wisdom."[11]

The Magic of the Runes

A second quest that Odin undertook to uncover secret knowledge involved finding certain potent magical powers. Ever since his birth, Odin had possessed an array of mystical abilities simply by virtue of being a divine being. He could heal the sick, for instance, cause people to fall in love, and change his shape at will. However, he was always trying to find new sources and types of magic. In this regard, he heard a rumor that several runes—letters of an unknown alphabet—lay hidden within the fabric of time and

runes
Letters of an old Germanic and Norse alphabet that legends claimed possessed magical properties

space. Moreover, as modern mythologist Mike Greenberg explains, "the lost alphabet was more than just a system of writing. Each symbol carried with it magic and when used in the correct way the runes could be used to weave powerful spells."[12] Odin became convinced that the runes could warp reality and make various aspects of the world look different than they were. Also, he believed, they would give him the ability to see into the near future.

The All-Father did not expect that gaining such powerful knowledge would be easy. He foresaw that, as had happened when he lost his eye, he would need to undergo some sort of painful sacrifice in exchange for expanding his powers. And hoping to increase his chances for success, he decided to inflict that pain on himself.

To that end, Odin traveled to the roots of Yggdrasil, the gigantic tree that the Norse believed encompassed the many realms of the world in its branches. There, he used his spear, called Gungnir, to stab himself in the abdomen; then he hung himself upside down from one of the great tree's roots. Bleeding, and without food or drink, he suffered day after day. However, his anguish did

An artist's vision of Yggdrasil, the World Tree, in which all creatures in the Norse worldview lived.

Odin and the Mead of Poetry

In addition to Odin's pursuits of knowledge from Mimir's well and the magical runes, in a third quest he sought the so-called gift of poetry. This boon would allow him to speak and write inspiring words. He was told that to gain those formidable abilities, he would need to drink a special liquid known as the Mead of Poetry. The only place in the known world where that drink could be found was a hidden cave in Jotunheim, the realm of the giants. Even though traveling in that land was dangerous for a god (because most giants despised the Aesir), Odin made the trip. Once there, he used his magical powers to excavate a tunnel through the side of a mountain. That passageway led to the hidden cave. And sure enough, in that cavern he found a keg containing the mead. Swiftly, the All-Father drank the container's contents and then returned to Asgard. His fellow gods were amazed at the degree of improvement in his speaking and writing abilities. And in a generous gesture, he later passed on those skills to several humans in the realm of Midgard. The Norse came to call them "Odin's gifts to humanity."

not go unnoticed. Greenberg points out that "some of the creatures that lived in the World Tree's branches approached him during his ordeal. The eagle in the tree's [branches] and the squirrel Ratatoskr watched his suffering but he forbade them from bringing him any food or water.[13]

Odin's torment lasted for nine days in total. Then, during the morning of the tenth day, his self-sacrifice paid off. The runes suddenly became visible, floating in air beside him, and he gratefully absorbed their powers. But because Odin was sacrificing himself to himself, the sacrificial Odin died, while the facet of his godhood that was receiving the sacrifice grew stronger. The results of this pivotal quest transformed him into a far more formidable deity than he had been before. In a sense, Greenberg continues, "a part of Odin died to give birth to the more exalted, powerful god who [possessed] the lost knowledge of runic magic." In this way, the Norse believed, the already supremely talented leader of their pantheon of gods "was reborn as a higher being."[14]

CHAPTER TWO

How Heimdall Helped Humanity

According to the captivating collection of myths left behind by the Norse, the chief god, Odin, had many sons. Among them was Heimdall, who was said to have had nine mothers. Exactly why and how this occurred remains mysterious, and modern scholars still debate it. What is more certain is that Heimdall oversaw the beneficial uses of fire. These included cooking food, providing heat in cold weather, and smelting metals to make tools and weapons.

Even more important in Heimdall's duties as a god, however, was his role as guardian of Bifrost, a bridge that connected Asgard, the realm of the gods, to Midgard, the land of humans. Also called the Rainbow Bridge, Bifrost's association with rainbows came from the fact that it was multicolored, although it was not semitransparent like a rainbow. Instead, it was a solid, very strong roadway. So the enemies of the gods, especially the giants from the realm of Jotunheim, could use it to enter and attack Asgard. It needed to be carefully guarded, therefore. And that duty fell to Heimdall.

As the events of countless centuries showed, Odin's son turned out to be the perfect choice to perform that crucial task. A diligent, multitalented being, Heimdall first constructed a huge, impregnable palace-fortress at the bridge's highest point, where it connected to Asgard. He called that impressive structure Himinbjorg, meaning "Heaven's Castle." Because of its lofty elevation, Heimdall had a magnificent panoramic view of large portions of Midgard. That allowed him to see any humans, giants, dwarfs, or other beings who were approaching Bifrost.

Also beneficial to Heimdall, and by extension the gods he protected, was the fact that he possessed the keenest senses of any living being in the known world. His vision was so good that he could see the residents of realms lying tens of thousands of miles away. And his hearing was so acute that he could hear grass growing. So there was no way that an enemy force could move through Midgard toward Bifrost without Heimdall detecting it.

And the gods were aware that just such an enemy force would eventually storm Bifrost and lofty Himinbjorg to destroy the Aesir. This was foretold in an ancient prophecy that predicted that thousands of giants and others who despised the gods would wage war against the Aesir and their human allies. That fateful conflict would result in Ragnarok, the final, furious battle for control of the universe. Furthermore, the prophecy said that Heimdall would play a key role in those events. Seeing the enemy's approach, he would mount his trusty steed Gulltoppr and blow his horn, called Gjallahorn, which could be heard throughout the world. That majestic sound would signal to the inhabitants of every realm that Ragnarok had come.

Gulltoppr
Heimdall's strong, faithful horse

Begetting the Slave Class

The tale of Heimdall's guardianship of Bifrost and participation in the apocalyptic battle of Ragnarok has been retold for at least thirteen centuries. Cited less often in Norse lore, yet by no means less important, are his contributions to humanity's development. Put simply, Heimdall is credited in the Norse myths with making a series of epic journeys to the human realm of Midgard. There, several medieval sources claim, he single-handedly created the social structure of human society.

Exactly why Heimdall decided to devote so much time and energy to helping the humans may never be known. There is some

Rig
The name Heimdall used when in disguise during his visits to Midgard

indication in the medieval sources that he felt sorry for humanity during its first few centuries of existence. People in Midgard seemed to fend for themselves without much thought for the needs of others. Also, no one was in charge of society, and few had any assigned roles or duties in the social order. As a result, human society never seemed to achieve anything worthwhile.

Determined to remedy this unfortunate situation, Heimdall disguised himself as a human because he wanted Midgard's residents to think that one of their own was making social improvements. Descending from Bifrost into Midgard, he trekked onward until he saw a modest-looking hut. When he knocked on the door, a middle-aged man and woman answered and introduced themselves as Ai (great-grandfather) and his wife, Edda (great-grandmother). Heimdall identified himself as Rig. He had traveled a long distance and was thirsty and hungry, he added.

In this image, Heimdall blows his horn, Gjallahorn. According to prophecy, he would one day blow that horn as a signal that Ragnarok had come.

Hearing that, the kindly couple invited him in and shared their supper with him.

Later, Ai and Edda also shared their bed with the stranger, who slept between them that night. Although Ai slept soundly throughout the night, that was not the case with Rig and Edda. This became apparent when nine months later she gave birth to a son, whom Edda named Thrall. Although physically unattractive, the boy turned out to be strong and extremely good at doing menial work. He subsequently married an unattractive but hardworking maiden named Thir the Drudge. And over time they produced many children, who in turn had their own children—all of whom seemed suited to feeding livestock, collecting firewood, and doing other low-skill labors. These offspring of Heimdall and Edda gave rise to the human social group called thralls.

The thralls, or slaves, were one of Viking culture's three main social classes. Members of the group had no legal rights and could be bought and sold like livestock. According to Daniel McCoy, there were three ways one might become a slave in Viking society:

> The first was simply to be born to a slave, since the children of slaves were also slaves. The second was to be captured in war. According to the ancient way of thinking, anyone who was captured in battle and whose life was spared had been given a tremendous gift, namely his life, which he had to pay back with an equally tremendous gift: his freedom. . . . The third way to become a slave was to go bankrupt. . . . An extremely poor but free person could give up his freedom to a better-off person in exchange for having his material needs taken care of.[15]

Karl and His Many Offspring

The Vikings also perpetuated a legendary tale that recounted Heimdall's second visit to Midgard. Journeying to a different section of that land, the story goes, the god, once again disguised as

Viking Warriors' Social Status

The tales describing Heimdall's expeditions into Midgard suggest that he established the hierarchy, or ladder, of Viking social classes, with thralls on the bottom rung and jarls on the top rung. However, Heimdall's myths were not specific about the place of Viking warriors in that hierarchy. As this society developed in real life, Norse fighters belonged to both the middle-class karls and the upper-class jarls. The difference was that the jarls who served as warriors tended to be the warlords who commanded the armies. And the ordinary fighters in the ranks were mostly karls. The slaves, or thralls, were normally not allowed to fight, although several of them carried weapons and supplies for their masters during wartime. The bulk of a typical fighting force was composed of free, young, unmarried men, karls who had little or no money and took up arms in hopes of gaining at least some modest amount of it. Sometimes that wealth was portable, in the form of silver, gold, or gems taken on raids. Other times it was in the form a plots of farmland given by the warlord in exchange for the karls' service.

the traveler Rig, visited the home of Afi (grandfather) and his wife, Amma (grandmother). As Ai and Edda had done, Afi and Amma fed Rig a hearty meal and shared their bed with him. And nine months later Amma gave birth to a son who received the name Karl. He was moderately attractive and a quick learner who became adept at plowing, raising livestock, and building houses and barns. He also had a head for figures, so he was competent at buying and selling goods.

Karl
The son born to the couple Afi and Amma after Heimdall visited them

Karl eventually married a free girl named Snor, much to the approval of Afi, who thought the young man was his own son. "Karl and Snor had a cluster of contented children," writes modern mythologist Kevin Crossley-Holland. "They called their first-born Hal, the Man, and their second, Dreng, the Warrior."[16] Another son was Smith, who turned out to be a skilled craftsman. Hal, Dreng, and Smith each had their own children, who in turn produced still more children. From these offspring of Heimdall and Amma arose the human social class called karls.

This story, for the residents of Scandinavia during the Viking age, explained how their second and biggest social class—the karls—originated. Unlike thralls, karls were free members of society who enjoyed full legal rights. That meant they could buy and sell land and other commodities, as well as become warriors if they wanted to. Although some karls did become fighters and made their living by raiding, most were farmers, merchants, and craftspeople, somewhat the equivalent of today's middle class.

Jarl: Born to Wield Power

It was a common belief among the medieval Norse that their highest social class first came about thanks to Heimdall's third visit to Midgard. The tale states that, as part of his overall plan to help humans, he approached a third human couple, consisting of Fathir and his wife, Mothir. They lived in a large, well-decorated house with many rooms. Fathir was an expert weapons maker, a trade that paid him handsomely, and Mothir was skilled at making beautiful clothes from the finest of fabrics.

Viking society had a number of classes. While the upper class did not have to work, the middle and lower classes did. Here, men work on a Viking ship.

Following the same traveling-Rig narrative, Heimdall got to know the couple and soon impregnated Mothir. Nine months later, she gave birth to a boy named Jarl. As he grew up, he proved to be extremely handsome and highly intelligent, and he easily learned new skills of various sorts. Also, people of all walks of life were drawn to him.

One day when he was about twenty, Jarl was walking in the forest near his home when he saw Rig—the family's friend—approaching. At first, they made some small talk. But then Rig's tone became more serious, and as Crossley-Holland relates, he told Jarl, "You are my son."[17] The young man now learned that Rig was not only his father but also the god Heimdall in disguise. Jarl was born to wield power and lead others, Heimdall explained, and must now go out and assert his control over the lower classes.

Inspired by learning his identity and potential, Jarl immediately began gathering loyal followers. In time, "he brought his followers to battle," Crossley-Howard says. "He slew warriors and won land. Before long, Jarl owned no less than eighteen halls [large buildings used for meetings and entertaining guests]. He won

Jarl's Many Halls

In the myth of Heimdall's quests to bring social order to humanity, the god's son Jarl is described as accumulating eighteen "halls." In medieval Viking society a hall was a building, or part of a building, where people gathered in large numbers for various reasons. These included meetings of members of the community, meals given by a jarl or other leader to loyal warriors or visiting dignitaries, trials to determine the fate of accused criminals, and/or religious and other annual celebrations. Not surprisingly, the largest halls were those of the jarls, today called earls, and, toward the latter part of the Viking age, regional kings and queens. However, some karls—the more successful merchants, for instance—had small halls of their own, where they entertained guests. Archaeologists have excavated the foundations and other remains of numerous Viking halls all over Scandinavia. The largest ones originally measured 160 to 180 feet (49 to 55 m) long and 30 to 50 feet (9 to 15 m) wide. Clearly, the fact that Heimdall's mythical son Jarl had eighteen halls indicates that he was an extremely rich and powerful leader.

great wealth."[18] Jarl also got married and had sons and grandsons, who were also well-to-do community leaders.

As in this popular myth, the jarls, or earls, in Norse society were wealthy and never had to do any hard labor, the way the thralls and karls did. Also, although some jarls were warriors, more often they were the warlords and commanders of ordinary fighters. Moreover, when a fourth, and very small, social class, consisting of kings and queens, developed late in the Viking age, the jarls remained powerful and influential as the nobles of those monarchs.

The journeys taken by Heimdall, disguised as the wanderer Rig, demonstrate how the Vikings' cherished myths often reflected the realities of their society. Most experts think that Rig's story was invented to explain where the Norse social classes came from. True or not, the tale is particularly insightful to people today who are fascinated by medieval Norse culture. As Crossley-Howard puts it, the myths of Rig's offspring provide "a detailed and colorful picture of the three classes—serf, peasant, and leader—into which society was divided throughout the Viking world."[19]

Thor's Adventures in Giant-Land

Thor, the Norse thunder god and wielder of a hammer that could crush mountain peaks, was concerned. He and his fellow Norse gods—the Aesir—were preparing to attend a feast that was to be held for them by Aegir, god of the seas. At the last minute, however, Aegir informed his would-be guests that he did not have a kettle large enough to brew the huge amount of ale that the divine beings would likely consume. Taking Thor aside, the sea deity asked him to find a proper kettle. As mythologist Hamilton W. Mabie tells the tale, Thor replied, "Of course I will. Only tell me where to get one."[20]

At first, it appeared that no one knew where to find a kettle of that size. But then Tyr, the god who oversaw warfare, spoke up. He said that his father, a giant named Hymir, had a massive ale kettle in his castle in Jotunheim, or Giant-Land. Thor retorted that he did not trust Hymir, or any other giant, to be hospitable enough to loan them the kettle. But Tyr said that if they were polite and nonthreatening, Hymir might well do it.

Grudgingly, Thor agreed to try. He and Tyr departed Asgard and journeyed to Hymir's fortress, where Hymir's mother greeted them. She had nothing against the Aesir, she said. But her son was not fond of them and might refuse to loan them such a valuable object. At that moment they heard Hymir approaching the front gate, and the giantess advised the two gods to hide inside one of Hymir's other massive brewing kettles.

It turned out that Hymir had a particularly acute sense of smell. And when he entered the castle, he immediately detected the two visitors and told them to show themselves. Thor and Tyr climbed out of their hiding place and wasted no time in asking Hymir to loan them his largest kettle. He was about to say no when he suddenly recognized his son, Tyr, and his fellow god Thor. Despite their huge difference in size, Hymir feared Thor because of his reputation as a giant killer. And to avoid a possible fight, Hymir agreed to loan him the kettle. According to Mabie, Tyr tried to lift the enormous object but failed. "Then Thor took the great pot in his hands and drew it up with such a mighty effort that his feet went through the stone floor of the hall, but he lifted it and, placing it on his head like a mighty helmet, walked off.[21]

The Potential Danger Posed by the Giants

Jotunheim's giants, called Jotnar (singular: Jotunn), are fascinating characters in Norse myths and lore. The god Thor's preoccupation with and frequent opposition to them also looms large in those tales. In fact, his quest for the ale-brewing kettle is only one of several adventurous journeys the thunder god made to the realm of the giants. One factor that tied all these forays together was that Thor bore an intense distrust of and dislike for giants. At first glance this seems strange, considering that his own mother, Jord, was a giant, and his father, Odin, also had a Jotunn for a mother.

Aegir, god of the seas, is pictured here brewing ale and hosting guests.

That made Thor three-quarters giant by lineage. And yet, for reasons that remain unclear, he always maintained a grudge against most giants.

Jord
Thor's mother, who was a giant from Jotunheim

Perhaps because Thor was a weather deity possessing deep connections with nature's fundamental forces, he may have sensed that the giants posed a potential danger to the gods and humans. This suspicion was based on a fact pointed out by modern mythologists that the Jotnar represent perilous natural forces such as fire, storms, earthquakes, and so forth. And as the god who sought to keep such forces under control, Thor was instinctively wary of giants. In his mind, most residents of Jotunheim (sometimes called Utgard) symbolized disorder and barbarism. In contrast, the gods and humans represented order and civilization. In Kevin Crossley-Holland's words, the bitterness between the gods and giants is in some ways a "conflict of good and evil. The gods embody aspects of natural and social order; the giants subvert that order and seek to overthrow it."[22]

Thor: From War Deity to Thunder God

Early forms of Thor were worshipped by the Germanic peoples of northern Europe as early as the first century CE. In his book the *Germania*, written in about 98 CE, the Roman historian Tacitus referenced Donar, a Germanic war god who was an early version of the Norse deity Thor. Confusing Donar with the semidivine Roman hero Hercules, Tacitus wrote:

> The Germans, like many other peoples, are said to have been visited by Hercules, and they sing of him as the foremost of all the heroes when they are about to engage in battle. They also have the well-known kind of chant . . . [to] terrify their foes. . . . [It is] a harsh, intermittent roar. And they hold their shields in front of their mouths, so that the sound is amplified into a deeper crescendo by the reverberation.

Over time, the Germanic peoples who settled in Scandinavia and became the Vikings came to emphasize not only Thor's skills as a warrior but also his abilities as a god of thunder and the weather. He was also seen as a deity of agriculture and fertility (so that his divine duties sometimes overlapped with those of the Norse fertility god Frey).

Quoted in Harold Mattingly, trans., *Tacitus: The "Agricola" and the "Germania."* New York: Penguin, 1970, p. 103.

That the Jotnar play so big a part in the Norse myths is also based on a belief in the literal existence of giants. Most people in medieval northern Europe, including the Vikings, were convinced that giants were real. The thirteenth-century Danish historian Saxo Grammaticus voiced this belief in his writings. He pointed to the many megalithic stone structures that dotted northern Europe, saying, "The fact that the land of Denmark was once inhabited by a race of giants is attested by the huge boulders found next to ancient burial mounds. . . . Anyone considering this wonder must reckon it unthinkable that ordinary human strength could lift such bulk."[23]

Jotunn
The Norse word for a member of a mythical race of giants; the plural is *Jotnar*

Skrymer's Offer

The reality of the Norse giants aside, the mythical Thor was undeniably preoccupied with them, and all his quests took place in Giant-Land. Of these, one of the more memorable was his colorful confrontation with an unusual giant named Utgard-Loki. That adventure began when the thunder god decided to explore a sector of Jotunheim he had never visited before. Taking along his young servant Thjalfi and the trickster god Loki (not to be confused with the giant), Thor traveled across Midgard, the realm of the humans, and eventually reached Giant-Land.

During their first day in Jotunheim, the three travelers came upon a large, extremely odd-shaped structure. It had a huge opening in the front that led into an equally big main room; from there, five round-shaped openings appeared to lead to other rooms. Before they could explore further, an apparent earthquake struck, making it hard for them to keep their balance. They exited the building and up ahead saw a truly enormous giant lying asleep on the ground. He was snoring, and each time he exhaled he twitched his arm, which caused another quake.

Utgard-Loki
A giant who ruled part of Jotunheim from his huge castle

According to Mabie's account, as the travelers approached the amazingly big being, he woke up with a start and stared at them. "Who are you?" Thor inquired. "I'm Skrymer," the giant replied. "But I don't need to ask your name. You are Thor. But what have you done with my glove?"[24] Thor and the others now realized that the strange structure they had earlier entered was Skrymer's glove.

The giant offered to join the travelers and guide them to the castle of Utgard-Loki, the ruler of that part of Jotunheim. Although Thor was wary of Skrymer, as he was of all giants, he did welcome the idea of a guide. So he agreed, and the four marched onward into the dense woodland.

In the late afternoon Skrymer announced that he was tired and needed to rest. And when Thor objected to stopping so soon, the giant told him to be quiet, laid down, and immediately fell asleep. Feeling insulted, Thor grew angry, grasped his mighty hammer, and smashed it down on Skrymer's forehead. To everyone's astonishment, however, the giant remained uninjured.

Belief That the Norse Giants Were Real

Most medieval northern Europeans, including the Vikings, believed that giants like those in the Norse myths were real beings. As proof, in his *Gesta Danorum* ("Deeds of the Danes"), the thirteenth-century Danish scholar Saxo Grammaticus singled out the many megalithic stone structures littering northern Europe. The individual stones in those monuments were simply too heavy for ordinary humans to lift and move, he wrote. Therefore, a race of giants must have once existed. Furthermore, he added, it was entirely possible that some of those huge creatures might still inhabit remote, mountainous areas. If anyone doubts whether these structures were raised "by superhuman power," he said,

> let him ponder the heights of certain mounds and then say, if he can, who carried such rocks to their tops. . . . Even on a level plain it would be difficult, and perhaps beyond your strength, to shift it. . . . Such creatures, as our compatriots maintain, are reckoned to inhabit the rugged and inaccessible wasteland . . . and to be endowed with transmutable [shape-shifting] bodies, so that they have the wonderous ability to appear and disappear, to be present and then suddenly somewhere else.

Quoted in Andy Orchard, *Dictionary of Norse Myth and Legend*. London: Cassell, 1997, p. 55.

This image shows Thor fighting giants. Thor bore an intense distrust of and dislike for giants.

Padraic Colum picks up the story, saying that Skrymer awakened and asked, "Did a leaf fall on my head?" As the others stared, open-mouthed, Skrymer fell back to sleep. Even angrier than before, Thor swung the hammer again. But once more, to his utter shock, the giant's head remained intact. This time after awakening, Skrymer asked, "Has an acorn fallen on my forehead?"[25]

Events Inside the Giant's Castle

The next morning the four travelers awoke early and continued their trek through the forest. Eventually, they reached a mostly treeless valley in which rose a towering stone fortress. Skrymer identified it as King Utgard-Loki's stronghold, wished the other three luck, and strolled off in a different direction.

Thor and his companions approached the castle's front gate and told the guards that they were tired and hungry and desired to receive the hospitality of the king. Utgard-Loki did invite them in. But before feeding them a meal, he said in a haughty tone of voice that the puny travelers must prove their worth in a series of contests. Fuming at being called "puny," Thor fought hard to contain his temper, for he reasoned he could meet any challenge a giant could devise.

In the first competition, Loki lost an eating contest to one of the king's soldiers. Next came an event in which the fleet-footed Thjalfi was defeated in a footrace by another of Utgard-Loki's followers. Then it was Thor's turn. In a drinking contest, he swallowed immense amounts of ale, and yet he was unable to consume as much as Utgard-Loki himself. Thor became suspicious, for he had never lost a drinking contest in his life.

The king did allow the visitors to stay overnight. The next morning, soon after they had departed the castle, they were surprised to see Utgard-Loki dash out the front gate and catch up to them. Mabie relates that now that the visitors were heading home, the king said, "I will tell you the truth." Utgard-Loki now admitted that he had beaten Thor "by deception, not by strength."[26] The king and the other giants had feared Thor and his destructive hammer, so Utgard-Loki had disguised himself as the giant Skrymer and used magic spells to trick the visitors into seeing things that were not real. When Thor had swung his hammer, he had actually destroyed entire mountaintops. Similarly, when in the castle, the giants had employed magic to cheat in the contests, which the visitors had actually won.

Hearing this confession, Thor could no longer quell his fury. He raised his hammer, intending to split the giant's skull in two. But in the next split second, Utgard-Loki suddenly vanished, presumably through more use of magic. The three travelers now returned to Asgard. But instead of bragging about his exploits in Giant-Land, as he usually did, this time Thor refused to speak about what had happened. Only Loki and Thjalfi knew the truth—that the purportedly invincible thunder god was too embarrassed to admit that a giant had outwitted him.

CHAPTER FOUR

Missions of the Divine Messengers

On what turned out to be a fateful morning for the Aesir, Skirnir, loyal messenger and trusted friend of the agricultural god Frey, awakened with the sunrise. After eating breakfast, Skirnir gathered Frey's servants, Byggvir and Beyla, and went to the spacious barn where the god kept his animals. As they did each morning, Byggvir and Beyla fed and groomed Frey's horses. Skirnir, meanwhile, saw to the needs of the god's most prized mount—the huge boar Gullinbursti.

Skirnir had just finished brushing the boar when Frey himself burst into the barn with vital news. Odin, leader of the gods, needed Skirnir immediately for a crucial mission, Frey said. This did not surprise Skirnir, because Odin often assigned him important tasks when Hermod, the Aesir's general messenger (and one of Odin's many sons), was not available.

When Skirnir asked Frey what was so urgent, the god explained that the giant wolf Fenrir, a monster that posed a threat to both the gods and humans, had been captured. Odin had ordered that the beast be chained and thereby immobilized. But that goal was proving difficult to meet. Odin, the war god Tyr, and others had tried to shackle the beast with chains composed of several different materials, and the great wolf had broken them all. As a last resort, therefore, Odin had decided to send a courier to Svartalfheim, realm of the dark elves, who were renowned for their inventive and industrial prowess. In Kevin Crossley-Holland's account of the myth, Odin had declared, "If anyone can make a fetter that will not break, the dark elves can."[27] Odin ordered his minions to go find Skirnir.

Only minutes later Skirnir reported to Odin. The All-Father stressed that time was short and that the mission must be completed as quickly as possible. To that end, Odin offered his own horse, the eight-legged and amazingly swift Sleipnir, and Skirnir wasted no time in galloping away.

The quest for an unbreakable chain took Skirnir out of Asgard and across Midgard's vast forests and mountain ranges. Braving storms, landslides, and banks of fog, he eventually made it to Svartalfheim. There, he sought out the master craftworkers Nar, Nain, Niping, and Nori, who dwelled in a deep, dark cavern. Skirnir offered them bags of gold in exchange for creating the special fetter, and "in the gloom," Crossley-Holland writes, their "eyes gleamed like glow-worms." They went right to work and only two days later presented Skirnir with a chain "as smooth and supple as a silk ribbon."[28]

When Skirnir returned to Asgard, he hurried to Odin and handed him the new shackle, which the dark elves had named Gleipnir. It was so thin it was barely visible. Yet it proved more than strong enough to bind the giant wolf. The grateful All-Father asked Skirnir what it was made of. And the answer, according

Fenrir is pictured here after being shackled by the gods. The dark elves created a chain that was thin and smooth but incredibly strong.

Loki's Ultimate Fate

After the other members of the Aesir found out about Loki's hand in Baldur's tragic death, they immediately sought to take him into custody. But they soon realized that he had fled Asgard. An exhaustive search followed, until they caught up with him on a secluded mountain peak on the far side of Jotunheim. There the trickster had been living in a small hunter's cottage near a waterfall that flowed into a stream. As the Aesir approached, Loki jumped into the stream and transformed himself into a fish. That ruse failed, however, because Odin and the others expected him to shape-shift to avoid detection.

After capturing him, they took him to a cave inside a mountain in Asgard and bound him in heavy iron chains. They placed a poisonous snake directly above his head, and that reptile dripped its caustic venom onto his face several times a day, causing him agonizing pain. Eventually, however, a prophecy saying that the forces of evil would destroy the Aesir came to pass. On the day of that fateful battle—called Ragnarok—Loki broke free, rushed out, and joined the evil ones. A few hours later he died in the fighting, in which Odin and most of the other gods perished as well.

to scholar Daniel McCoy, was a mixture of "the sound of a cat's footsteps, a woman's beard, the roots of a mountain, a bear's tendons, a fish's breaths, and the spittle of a bird."[29]

The Spirit of Social Communication

All the gods wondered at how something composed of such insubstantial elements could be so strong. At the same time Odin marveled that Skirnir had traveled so far on what could well have been an impossible mission. The All-Father often privately told fellow deities how fortunate the Aesir were to have beings as valuable as Skirnir and Hermod in their midst.

Those heavenly messengers were indeed multitalented entities who carried out a host of logistical duties for the divine residents of Asgard. The two were sometimes called on to be skilled diplomats charged with convincing friends and enemies alike to do the Aesir's bidding. They were also enormously brave individuals who repeatedly risked injury and their very lives to complete their missions and quests. In addition, in the legendary Norse universe of the vast World Tree and its diverse inhabitants, Skirnir and Hermod were key figures who personified the spirit of social communication. Without the knowledge and information that they carried among the World Tree's realms and races, distrust, chaos, and destructive wars would surely have been more frequent.

Moreover, other information-bearing beings fulfilled similar roles in the Norse myths. For instance, in his collection of stories about Norse heroes and kings, the thirteenth-century Icelandic writer Snorri Sturluson said of Odin, "Two ravens sit on his shoulders and whisper all the news which they see and hear into his ear; they are called Huginn and Muninn. He sends them out in the morning to fly around the whole world, and by breakfast they are back again. Thus, he finds out many new things."[30]

Huginn and Muninn
The two ravens that daily gathered news of the world for Odin

That the two birds bore humanlike intelligence is shown by their names. *Huginn* means "thought," and *Muninn* usually translates as "memory." In a very real sense, modern scholars suggest, they were extensions of Odin's own information-packed mind. As McCoy puts it, they were "Odin's intellectual/spiritual capabilities journeying outward in the form of fittingly intelligent and curious birds."[31] That is, Odin sent out spiritual aspects of himself to gather additional information and thereby expand his store of wisdom.

A Quest in the Name of Love

Although Odin's ravens were valuable to him as information gatherers, they were not nearly as versatile as the divine messengers. Skirnir and Hermod could—and often did—negotiate and make deals with a wide variety of beings worldwide. A well-known example was the lengthy journey Skirnir undertook at the bequest of his lovesick friend, Frey.

The god who oversaw soil fertility became thoroughly smitten by a woman one day when Odin was away from Asgard. Out for a morning stroll, Frey passed by the staircase leading upward to the so-called High Seat—Odin's throne. From that enchanted chair, which gave telescopic vision to whoever sat on it, the All-Father could see almost all the world's realms.

Skirnir rode to Jotunheim, where he found Gerd and persuaded her to meet Frey.

Frey had always wanted to witness that wondrous view. And figuring that Odin would never find out, he climbed the stairs and sat in the High Seat. The vista was every bit as spectacular as Frey had imagined. He could easily make out Midgard and beyond it the icy summits of the mountains in Giant-Land. It was on a slope of one of those peaks that he suddenly caught sight of an incredibly beautiful woman. In that moment he held his breath, struck by an overpowering feeling that his fate was to marry her.

Barely able to contain his excitement, Frey hurried down the stairs and summoned his faithful friend and messenger. In mythologist Brian Branston's account, when Skirnir arrived, the god described what he had seen and exclaimed, "Since I saw her from Odin's High Seat I cannot live without her. And now that you are here, I want you to ride to Jotunheim and demand her hand in marriage for me."[32]

Skirnir Brings Good News

The late mythologist Hamilton W. Mabie became well known for his charming retellings of the Norse myths. The following is part of his description of what happened after Skirnir returned from Jotunheim with the good news that Gerd had agreed to come to Asgard:

> Skirnir was soon mounted and riding homeward as fast as his horse could carry him. He was so happy in the thought of Frey's happiness that the distance seemed short, and as he drew near he saw Frey standing before his [castle], looking anxiously for his coming. "She is yours!" he shouted, urging his horse into swifter flight. . . . The days that followed were long enough for Frey; but even the longest day comes to an end, and at last the ninth day came. Never sun shone so brightly or south wind blew so musically as on the morning when . . . under the branches of the great trees, Frey found the beautiful Gerd waiting for his coming. . . . And the whole earth was happy in them, for while they stood with clasped hands the skies grew soft . . . the ripening grain swayed in the fields, and summer lay warm and fragrant over the land.

Heritage History, "Norse Stories Retold from the Eddas by H.W. Mabie: The Wooing of Gerd," 2023. www.heritage-history.com.

Although Skirnir had his doubts that someone could fall in love at first sight, out of steadfast loyalty he did his duty. After hastily gathering some provisions, he mounted a fast horse and sped away overland. The journey took several days, and both horse and rider were exhausted when they reached Jotunheim. Yet they pressed on, without resting, for several more days until they entered the village where the woman lived. Approaching her, Skirnir introduced himself and soon learned that her name was Gerd. Although her parents were giants, she was of the same height and stature as Frey and the other gods.

At first, Gerd said that she had no desire to go to distant Asgard and marry someone she had never met. But Skirnir repeatedly cajoled, pressed, and enticed her until she eventually agreed to at least meet the god who had viewed her from afar. As it turned out, when Gerd arrived in Asgard, she instantly fell in love with Frey, and the two were married a few days later.

Gerd
The beautiful maiden Frey saw from afar and fell in love with

Hermod Gives His All

In the years that followed, Skirnir remarked more than once how fortunate he was to have been given a mission that ended so happily. Such was not the case, however, for Hermod's most famous quest. His mission was triggered by a prominent death rather than the power of love. The lost life was that of Baldur, god of light and virtue and a son of Odin. One day several of the gods gathered in a meadow to play games, and during the festivities Baldur suddenly fell dead. Initially, it appeared that his brother Hodur, god of winter, had intentionally slain Baldur. But soon the other Aesir discovered that Loki, deity of deceit, was the real culprit.

Moreover, an unwelcome reality intensified the grief felt by the gods and millions of humans. Baldur's mother, Frigg, goddess of marriage, said his noble spirit had been snatched by Hel, queen of the kingdom of the dead. As a result, Baldur's soul was now trapped in that gloomy subterranean realm, called Helheim. Frigg and Odin were determined to get Baldur's essence back so it could rest peacefully in Asgard. And to that end they dispatched the messenger Hermod to reason with the thoroughly unpleasant Hel.

For the crucial task, Hermod was allowed to use Odin's trusty steed Sleipnir, the fastest horse in existence. That magnificent animal carried the stalwart rider across the plains, mountain ranges, and rivers of several continents until they neared Yggdrasil's

Frigg, goddess of marriage, is pictured here. After her son Baldur died and was taken to the land of the dead, Frigg and Odin sent Hermod to get Baldur's essence back so it could rest peacefully in Asgard.

The True Villain of the Story

Hel, queen of the realm of the dead, Helheim, is often described as the villain of the story of the fight to free Baldur's soul. But as many modern scholars have pointed out, her refusal to release Baldur's spirit was to be expected, given her miserable, at times mean-spirited nature. The true villain of the story, the experts contend, is the trickster god Loki, who secretly disliked his fellow divinities. Indeed, it was Loki who convinced Hodur, deity of winter and darkness, to throw a spear at the invulnerable Baldur. Hodur fully expected the missile to bounce off his brother. Unknown to all present, including Hodur, was that Loki had placed poison on the spear's tip, which allowed it to penetrate Baldur's body and kill him. Compounding this crime, later, when Hel announced her ultimatum that all beings and objects must weep for Baldur, Loki caused more mischief. Disguising himself as a giant named Thokk, he refused to cry for Baldur, thereby sealing the doom of Baldur's noble spirit.

massive roots. Then, in Crossley-Holland's words, "for nine nights Hermod rode through a valley so deep and dark that he was unable to see anything. The ground fell away from him and the cold fingers of the underworld began to reach up towards him."[33]

Finally reaching the vast, murky caverns of Helheim, valiant Hermod stood before that realm's ruler. In the name of Odin and the other Aesir, he said, Hel must release Baldur's spirit immediately. With a sneer, however, the ghastly queen of death refused. Only if every being and object in the universe cried for Baldur, she declared, would she comply.

Thokk
A giant who refused to cry for Baldur's noble spirit

In the days that followed, one after another of the world's residents and objects did indeed weep for Baldur. There was one holdout, however—a giant named Thokk. And so Hel kept Baldur's soul imprisoned in her gloomy realm, to the sorrow of untold millions. Of those, very possibly no one was sadder than Hermod, who had given his all in what Odin later called a truly noble effort to do the right thing.

CHAPTER FIVE

The Search for a Lost Sister

The people who lived in Hvalsey, a Norse settlement on the western coast of Greenland, gathered in the village center. All were excited because word had spread that the formidable Thorbjorg would be arriving soon. She was well known throughout the westernmost Viking settlements for two reasons, the first being that she frequently spent the winter traveling from place to place. Second, she was said to be a seeress, a female who possessed certain magical abilities to foretell the future. With a touch of awe, many people called her the "Little Prophetess."

Thorbjorg
A legendary prophetess who traveled through the Norse villages in western Greenland

Everyone in Hvalsey knew that Thorbjorg had been summoned by Thorkell Farserkur. The owner of the largest farm in the district, Thorkell, like his neighbors, was concerned about the famine that had ravaged the region for two seasons. Would it continue? Or would it soon abate? Hopefully, he reasoned, the highly respected Little Prophetess would be able to enlighten Hvalsey's worried residents.

Suddenly, someone spotted Thorbjorg approaching, accompanied by a mix of male and female traveling companions. She wore a black mantle—a loose, sleeveless jacket—crisscrossed with a leather strap embedded with small colored stones. Around her neck was a string of glass beads, and she wore a black lambskin hood atop her head. In her right hand she gripped a walking stick with a roundish knob at the top, and she carried a big leather purse in her left hand. Rounding out her impressive outfit were calfskin boots lined with fur, and gloves made of catskin, also lined with fur.

Once the visitors and the villagers had gathered near Thorkell's farm, Thorbjorg stepped forward and extended a formal greeting. Then she explained that she required the assistance of a woman who knew the words of an ancient song said to summon the spirits of the dead. A young maiden named Gudrid stepped forward and said she had learned that song as a child. According to the medieval work known as *The Saga of Erik the Red*, Thorbjorg sat in a chair provided by Thorkell.

> Then sang Gudrid the [song] in so beautiful and excellent a manner, that to no one there did it seem that he had ever before heard the song in voice so beautiful as now. [Thorbjorg] thanked her for the song. "Many spirits," said she, "have been present under its charm, and were pleased to listen to the song. . . . And now are many things clear to me which before were hidden both from me and others. And I am able this to say, that the [famine] will last no longer, the season improving as spring advances."[34]

Having prophesied a positive future for the area, Thorbjorg gathered her entourage and departed. The thankful Thorkell remarked that she was destined to travel onward and visit distant lands. Moreover, the Little Prophetess could be trusted always to use her magic for good rather than evil.

Mixed Views About Using Magic

Select individuals like Thorbjorg, who supposedly possessed magical powers, were not uncommon in Norse society. Some of them female, others male, they were influential because of a general belief that the world was filled with potent supernatural forces. In addition to mystical beings like the gods, giants, and elves, purportedly there was magic itself, called *seid*. Widely accepted as a real phenomenon, it was thought to have diverse uses. According to archaeologist Neil S. Price:

seid
Magic, or the ability to perform supernatural spells

> There were seid rituals for divination and clairvoyance [foretelling the future]; for seeking out the hidden, both in the secrets of the mind and in physical locations; for healing the sick; for bringing good luck; for controlling the weather; for calling game animals and fish. Importantly, it could also be used for the opposite of these things—to curse an individual or an enterprise; to blight the land and make it barren; to induce illness; to tell false futures . . . [and] to injure, maim and kill.[35]

Seers possessed magical powers. Here, Odin consults a seer.

The Norse had mixed views about using magic. Some felt that it was effeminate, or unmanly, to cast spells or contact the spirits of the dead. Therefore, they believed that such activities should be engaged in solely by seeresses like Thorbjorg. This belief seemed to ignore the fact that the universally revered god Odin himself practiced magic from time to time.

Other Vikings accepted that men could practice seid, but only for good. If magic was used for malicious or criminal reasons, it was widely accepted that the perpetrator—whether female or male—deserved to be killed. That Thorbjorg was admired throughout the western Norse settlements, rather than condemned and executed, indicates that she used her alleged powers only in positive ways.

Formidable Offspring in a Legendary Era

The annals of Norse mythology contain the story of another character who traveled extensively and possessed magical powers. That controversial figure's name was Nor, and the most detailed

Was King Fornjot the Original Norse Giant?

The Vikings and other medieval northern Europeans believed that their ancestor, King Fornjot, was a giant. Moreover, some of the Norse storytellers who perpetuated this myth suggested that Fornjot was not just any giant; rather, he was the very first giant—and indeed the first thinking being—in the universe. The Norse called that huge creature Ymir. Supposedly, he had been formed from a big blob of warm water that was infused with various unknown magical qualities. Initially, according to the main Norse creation myth, Ymir did nothing but sleep for untold numbers of centuries. Eventually, however, he awakened when he felt weird lumps forming inside one of his armpits. These bulges grew into smaller versions of Ymir himself and became the first members of the race of giants that lived in the realm of Jotunheim according to the Norse myths. Ultimately, in the primary Norse creation story, the god Odin slew Ymir. But minor alternate versions of the story evolved over time, including one in which Ymir survived and became King Fornjot.

version of his story appears in the *Orkneyinga Saga*, a Norse document written in about 1200 CE. The complex tale begins in the dimly remembered past, well before the historical Viking Age (roughly 800 to 1050 CE) began. At the time, Nor's ancestor, King Fornjot, ruled a large section of what is now Finland.

What made Fornjot unusual was his size. Exactly how large he was is lost in the mists of time, but later generations of Finlanders said he was a giant. In fact, some rumors claimed he may have been the primordial giant Ymir, who magically created the race of giants who opposed the Norse gods.

Whatever the truth about Fornjot may have been, he fathered many generations of extremely formidable offspring, all known for being unusually tall, strong, courageous, and ambitious. One of his sons, Kari (a name meaning "storm"), had a son named Frosti ("frost"), who in turn fathered a boy named Snaer ("snow"). Snaer's own son, Thorri, was said to have had interactions with various Norse gods, possibly including Odin, in that legendary era. Also, as descendants of a mystical primeval giant, Thorri and his ancestors all retained varying degrees of seid, which allowed them to cast spells and do other forms of magic.

Goi
An early Finnish princess who disappeared, prompting her brothers to search for her

The Disappearance of a Princess

Perhaps because of his relationships with some of the gods, Thorri was a very religious monarch who held large-scale public sacrifices every winter. And when his three children were old enough, he taught them to help run those ceremonies. In their first attempts, the two sons, Nor and Gor, excelled. Then it came time for the daughter, Goi, to take her turn. But on the day of the sacrifice, to the surprise of family and friends alike, she was nowhere to be found. The worried Thorri ordered his soldiers to thoroughly search every village and farm in the kingdom. And he and his sons may well have used their magical abilities to cast spells that would aid in that endeavor. But it was all to no avail, as no one could find a trace of the princess.

In time, the king decided he had no choice but to call off the search for Goi. But her brothers refused to give up. Nor and Gor told their father that there was a good chance that some unknown foreigner may have abducted their sister. And they had decided to go on a long-distance quest to find her. Furthermore, the brothers split up and mounted separate expeditions to cover more ground.

Gor commanded three ships, which sailed through and searched the many islands lying along Scandinavia's long coastline. Meanwhile, Nor traveled on foot westward across what are now northern Sweden and Norway. He systematically went from village to village in that sprawling, often snow-covered area, but he was unable to unearth any leads, so he pivoted southward into the central Norwegian region of Trondheim.

A man reads the position of sticks cast to divine the future. Norse society believed in the existence of magic and occult powers.

A Mangled Memory of Real Events?

Modern historians have repeatedly shown that some ancient myths had a basis in actual historical events. An often-cited example is the famous Trojan War, in which a coalition of ancient Greek kings sacked the mercantile city of Troy. Modern archaeologists proved that Troy was a real city (in what is now Turkey) that did undergo attacks, although the exact identity of the attackers is still debated. Similarly, some scholars suggest, the myth of King Thorri's sons, Nor and Gor, and Nor's establishment of the first large Norwegian kingdom may be a mangled memory of the folk migrations of early Scandinavian peoples. Evidence shows that Germanic tribes moved northward and settled in parts of southern Scandinavia in the late first millennium BCE and early first millennium CE, and those groups eventually morphed into various Norse-speaking peoples. By the early 700s CE, what is now Norway was made up of several separate Norse chiefdoms or kingdoms. It is possible that one of them may have been founded by Norse speakers from what is now Finland. If so, the western migration of that group might have given rise to the legend of Nor's travels and conquests.

It was in Trondheim that Nor reunited with Gor, and the two brothers added a second goal to their ongoing travels. As historian C. Keith Hansley points out, although they "had originally begun their journeys to search for their sister, they quickly were distracted by the idea of conquest." Moreover, thanks to the magical abilities they had inherited from their ancestors, they were able to employ spells that made the inhabitants of towns and villages more likely to obey their commands. As a result, Hansley continues, "by the time Nor reached Trondheim Fjord [an inland waterway fed by the sea], a large army of followers were drawn to the wanderer's strength. Nor sent these followers out to scout for his sister—if these spies faced resistance from a settlement, Nor would conquer the obstinate region and expand his domain."[36]

Nor's Forceful Way

Aided by his brother, Nor continued his conquests in central Scandinavia for a few more years. At one point, word came from some of his soldiers that they had located his sister Goi further south, in the town of Heidemark. Hearing this, Nor and Gor hurried there and were reunited with her. She explained that a prominent warrior named Hrolf had kidnapped her years before. At first, she said, she had wanted to escape. But over time she had fallen in love with Hrolf, and now they were happy together.

In spite of Goi's insistence that she was content where she was, Nor was angry that she had been abducted in the first place. He challenged Hrolf to a duel. It was no ordinary fight, however. It turned out that Hrolf also possessed magical abilities inherited from supernatural ancestors. And when the two men clashed in single combat, using mystical spells as weapons, neither could best the other. Evenly matched, they decided to make peace. Nor later married Hrolf's sister (whose name has not survived), and Nor opted to spend the rest of his life in the nearby kingdom he had recently forged. Many of its locals remarked that the realm had formed thanks to the forceful "way" Nor had seized control of it. Hence, they came to call it Norway, which over time became one of Europe's greatest countries.

CHAPTER SIX

Saga of the Legendary Ragnar

In the mysterious mists of northern Europe's early medieval period, the names Harald Fairhair and Eric Bloodaxe once loomed large. Myths from that era say that Harald united about twenty Norwegian chiefdoms in about 872 CE and thereby established the nation of Norway. During the last few years of his reign, the story goes, he favored and shared power with his most famous son, Eric Haraldsson, nicknamed Eric Bloodaxe. This was the king's attempt to groom Eric to take the throne upon Harald's death.

Harald had many other sons, however. And they all wanted their shares of political power in Norway. So, after the father died, there was a period of civil unrest in which Eric fought, defeated, and killed several of his male siblings. This bloodbath, according to the legends, is what earned Eric the nickname Bloodaxe. Supposedly, he was a savage and power-hungry individual who had no qualms about literally cutting his enemies to pieces. Yet he was also known for his bravery, and to most of the Norse fighters of the Viking age he was often seen as a heroic figure as well as an uncompromising and violent one.

According to the Norse sagas—compilations of a mix of history and myth penned in the 1300s—and other medieval documents, Eric eventually attacked parts of the British Isles. That included taking over the Anglo-Saxon kingdom of Northumbria (in what is now northern England). A few years later, however, King Eadred, ruler of another British kingdom—Wessex—invaded Northumbria and drove Eric and his Vikings out. Subsequently, in about 954 Eric was slain in battle, possibly in southern Scotland. According to *Eiriksmal*, an anonymous poem about him written shortly after his demise, the chief Norse god Odin was excited when he heard that Eric's spirit would soon arrive in Valhalla. Odin supposedly asked a fellow deity:

> What kind of dream is this, that I had thought before daybreak I was preparing Valhalla for a slain army? I awakened the *einherjar* [the souls of other dead warriors inhabiting Valhalla], asking them to get up to [lay out] the benches and to rinse the drinking cups. I asked the Valkyries [divine warrior women who carried the heroes' spirits to Valhalla] to bring [extra] wine, as if a leader should come.[37]

Deeds Either Fabricated or Exaggerated

It is only natural to ask why Harald Fairhair and Eric Bloodaxe, who until recent times were thought to be real historical figures, are prominent characters in Norse mythology. Part of the answer is that the Vikings who lived during the 900s to 1100s CE often incorporated real people from their past into their myths. Typically, the actual deeds of such individuals had been majorly exaggerated and embellished over time. And that process had turned what had been real events into legendary ones.

Harald Fairhair
A legendary warrior-king said to have united many separate chiefdoms into the nation of Norway

Furthermore, some of the mythical characters who were thought to have once been authentic people had *not* actually been real. For example, various medieval Norse documents talk about Harald as if he were real. But modern scholars have concluded that he was semifictional, if not totally fabricated. First, most of the writings about his life did not appear until nearly three centuries after his death. Also, they tend to contradict one another. Hence, experts say, his image and supposed deeds were likely based on stories that had been

Harald Fairhair, pictured here, was said to have established the nation of Norway.

simply made up to explain how the early Norwegian chiefdoms became united.

As for Harald's renowned son, Eric, historians think he may have been real. But most of the deeds attributed to him were probably fictitious or at least highly exaggerated. Norwegian journalist Daniel Albert points out, "As is the case with many historical figures of that time period, we know little about what he did, and what we do know is clouded in uncertainty. Few Viking sagas tell us about him, and the ones that do don't agree with each other."[38]

Part of the problem with interpreting those works is that the Norse peoples who lived during the Viking age had no accurate written histories. Instead, they relied on legends about various heroes and villains of the past, both divine and human, and assumed that their stories were largely true. In this way, on the one hand some made-up characters were accepted as real. And on the other, over time several real historical people developed into bigger-than-life characters whose stories blended with older myths about gods, giants, and elves.

In addition to Eric Bloodaxe, the Vikings celebrated several other real human heroes whose deeds were either made up or highly exaggerated. Of those accounts, by far the most famous

Eric Bloodaxe, pictured here, was the son of Harald Fairhair and a prominent character in Norse mythology.

and most often recited are those describing a hero of epic proportions. His name was Ragnar Lothbrok. The best-known and most detailed source describing his life and deeds is an anonymous thirteenth-century Icelandic work titled *The Saga of Ragnar Lothbrok*.

As is the case with Harald Fairhair, it is likely that Ragnar was not a real person. Or at least most of Ragnar's supposed deeds were invented or embellished. And yet he became an incredibly renowned Viking hero. Utrecht University scholar Emma Groeneveld sums up Ragnar's mythical image, saying:

> As far as we know, there was no one historical person that matches his alleged deeds . . . to any proper degree. It is more likely that in the centuries after the adventurous 9th-century Viking heyday of raids, stories cropped up to unify various historical events and known persons under one roof. Several historians have indeed argued that Ragnar Lothbrok may be an amalgam [combination] of various historical figures, tied together into one mythical hero who was the scourge [menace] of 9th-century CE northern Europe.[39]

Dragonslayer and Frequent Husband

It is important to emphasize that the legendary Ragnar was a scourge only to his enemies. He had numerous followers and admirers in many parts of Scandinavia and beyond who viewed him as a hero of the first order. His often dangerous adventures began when he was still a young man, likely in his early twenties. The son of Denmark's King Sigurd Ring, it was said that the prince was

Weapons Used by Ragnar and His Soldiers

Norse legends claim that Ragnar Lothbrok's favorite weapon was the battle-ax, consisting of a large ax-head attached to a wooden pole measuring 3 feet (91 cm) or more in length. But he was also known to be quite skilled with swords, spears, and other offensive weapons commonly employed by the Vikings during the 700s to 900s CE. Others included daggers, bows and arrows, and lances. The Vikings of Ragnar's era also utilized several defensive devices, including metal helmets and on occasion chain mail (made up of numerous small iron rings sewn onto a jacket made of leather or multiple layers of fabric). Particularly effective were Viking shields. Most were circular or oval, made of wood, and featured a metal plate or knob, called a boss, in the center to help protect the hand that held the shield. The wooden parts of most shields have disintegrated over the centuries. But in 2008 archaeologists in Sweden unearthed an almost completely intact shield dating to the 900s CE—the height of the Viking Age.

both handsome and well trained as a warrior. Supposedly, he was particularly skilled at using a battle-ax.

According to Ragnar's myth, he got his first chance to demonstrate those martial abilities by fighting and killing a bear and a large, vicious dog at the same time. Shortly thereafter he married the first of his at least three wives—a shield maiden, or female warrior, named Lagertha. He soon divorced her, however, because of an opportunity he apparently felt he could not pass up. After his father died and left him the kingdom, a Swedish nobleman, Herraud by name, made a public announcement. The pet snake of his daughter, Thora, he said, had rapidly grown into a large, frightening dragon. And he vowed that whoever was able to slay the beast would receive Thora's hand in marriage.

Thora
Ragnar Lothbrok's second wife, whose pet snake grew into a frightening dragon

Ragnar recognized the chance to instantly gain widespread fame. After accepting the challenge, the young prince went to Sweden and tracked down the monster. According to one of several medieval documents that describe Ragnar, as soon as the creature "saw that a stranger had come, it reared up and blew poison at him. But he [Ragnar] thrust his shield at it and went bravely towards it and pierced its heart with his spear. Then he drew his sword and cut off the serpent's head."[40]

Impressed by Ragnar's good looks and obvious bravery, Thora gladly wedded Ragnar. Later, after she died of an unknown illness, he met and married a Norwegian farm girl named Aslaug. Contradictions in some of the medieval tales about Ragnar have made it difficult to tell which wife birthed which of his many children. He had at least nine offspring, including three sons—Bjorn Ironside, Ivar the Boneless, and Sigurd Snake-in-the-Eye—who would achieve their own fame as leaders and raiders.

From Conquests to Capture

During the years when Ragnar's children were growing up, his fondness for challenges and adventure led him to raise Norse

After Thora died, Ragnar married Aslaug, pictured here. Altogether he had at least nine children.

armies and invade neighboring lands. As a result, little by little he brought most of Sweden and Norway under his control. That made him, by now possibly in his late forties, one of the most famous Vikings of his time or any other.

Ragnar's next target was England. He told his leading followers that he would first capture the kingdom of Northumbria and then move on to the other English realms. So self-assured had he become by this time that he bragged he would subdue all of England with only enough soldiers to fill two ships.

This attitude proved grossly overconfident, however. When Northumberland's ruler, King Aella, heard about the approaching invaders, he mustered a large army. As a medieval document states, he soon "marched against Ragnar with an overwhelming host,

Aella
King of the English realm of Northumbria, who captured and executed Ragnar Lothbrok

The Blood-Eagle: Real or Literary Invention?

According to Ragnar's famous myth, when his sons learned that he had been executed by Northumbria's King Aella, they were furious. They were also horrified that their father had been thrown into a pit filled with venomous vipers. Swearing to achieve vengeance for Ragnar, three of the sons, including Ivar the Boneless, amassed a large force and invaded Northumbria. Ragnar's myth states that after they defeated Aella, they captured him and executed him using a gruesome Viking method known as the blood-eagle. It consisted of first slicing open the victim's back and separating the ribs from the spine. Next, the executioner pulled the bones and skin outward, creating what looked like a set of wings. Finally, often with the victim still alive and screaming, he reached in and removed the lungs from the chest cavity. The problem with this account of Aella's demise is that many modern historians doubt it happened. First, the English chronicles that mention Aella claim he died in battle. Second, no human remains from that period having the ribs detached in that manner have ever been found. It may be, those scholars say, that the blood-eagle was an invention of medieval storytellers and was never actually performed.

and [a] hard and terrible battle ensued. . . . The defending army was so big that nothing could withstand them, so almost all his [Ragnar's] men were killed, but he himself charged four times through the ranks of King [Aella]. . . . Finally he [Ragnar] was taken captive."[41]

Aella wanted to terrify his prisoner and make him beg for mercy. To that end, the Northumbrian king had Ragnar thrown into a pit filled with poisonous snakes. Aella and his followers must have been shocked and angry when their captive faced death unafraid, defiant, and with moving dignity. "The gods will invite me in," Ragnar purportedly stated, referring to his soul ascending to the heaven of fallen warriors, Valhalla. "The hours of life have passed," he quipped, smiling, "and laughing shall I die."[42]

The Exemplary Viking Warrior

Ragnar's laughing in the face of death inspired all Vikings who subsequently told and retold his story and strengthened their pride as a people. They also found a specific part of the tale particularly gratifying. It was when some of Ragnar's sons eventually captured Aella and tortured him to death.

Did most of Ragnar's larger-than-life adventures really happen? Probably no one will ever know for sure. Yet his legendary image, frequently embellished over the centuries, has become that of the quintessential Viking warrior. His name "resounds across the ages," says Luciano Anastasi, an expert on medieval Europe. "His ferocity in battle, his strategic genius, and his relentless pursuit of conquest have solidified his place as a Viking hero and a revered figure in Viking lore. Ragnar's legacy endures, inspiring awe and fascination, as his legendary persona continues to captivate the imagination of those who seek to unravel the enigmatic tapestry of Viking history."[43]

SOURCE NOTES

Introduction: An Adventurous People

1. Quoted in Daniel McCoy, *The Viking Spirit: An Introduction to Norse Mythology and Religion*. Self-published, CreateSpace Independent Publishing Platform, 2016, p. 266.
2. Quoted in McCoy, *The Viking Spirit*, p. 268.
3. Quoted in McCoy, *The Viking Spirit*, pp. 269–70.
4. Visit Norway, "Norwegian Vikings," 2024. www.visitnorway.com.
5. H.R.E. Davidson, *Scandinavian Mythology*. New York: Peter Bedrick, 1986, p. 213.

Chapter One: The All-Father's Quests for Wisdom

6. Quoted in Carolyne Larrington, trans., *The Poetic Edda*. New York: Oxford University Press, 2014, p. 40.
7. Quoted in Larrington, *The Poetic Edda*, pp. 45–46.
8. Quoted in John Lindow, *Handbook of Norse Mythology*. Oxford, UK: ABC-CLIO, 2001, p. 164.
9. Quoted in Padraic Colum, *The Children of Odin*. New York: Macmillan, 1934, p. 83.
10. Quoted in Colum, *The Children of Odin*, p. 83.
11. Colum, *The Children of Odin*, p. 84.
12. Mike Greenberg, "Odin's Discovery of the Runes," Mythology Source, November 9, 2020. https://mythologysource.com.
13. Greenberg, "Odin's Discovery of the Runes."
14. Greenberg, "Odin's Discovery of the Runes."

Chapter Two: How Heimdall Helped Humanity

15. Daniel McCoy, "The Viking Social Structure," Norse Mythology for Smart People. https://norse-mythology.org.
16. Keven Crossley-Holland, *The Norse Myths*. New York: Pantheon, 1980, p. 21.
17. Quoted in Crossley-Holland, *The Norse Myths*, p. 24.
18. Crossley-Holland, *The Norse Myths*, p. 24.
19. Crossley-Holland, *The Norse Myths*, pp. 189–90.

Chapter Three: Thor's Adventures in Giant-Land

20. Quoted in Hamilton W. Mabie, *Norse Mythology: Great Stories from the Eddas*. Mineola, NY: Dover, 2015, p. 42.
21. Mabie, *Norse Mythology*, p. 46.

22. Crossley-Holland, *The Norse Myths*, p. 185.
23. Quoted in Andy Orchard, *Dictionary of Norse Myth and Legend*. London: Cassell, 1997, p. 55.
24. Quoted in Mabie, *Norse Mythology*, p. 65.
25. Quoted in Colum, *The Children of Odin*, p. 112.
26. Quoted in Mabie, *Norse Mythology*, p. 71.

Chapter Four: Missions of the Divine Messengers

27. Quoted in Crossley-Holland, *The Norse Myths*, p. 35.
28. Crossley-Holland, *The Norse Myths*, p. 35.
29. McCoy, *The Viking Spirit*, p. 174.
30. Quoted in Rudolf Simek, *Dictionary of Northern Mythology*, trans. Angela Hall. Cambridge, UK: Brewer, 1993, p. 164.
31. Daniel McCoy, "Hugin and Munin," Norse Mythology for Smart People. https://norse-mythology.org.
32. Quoted in Brian Branston, *Gods and Heroes from Viking Mythology*. New York: Peter Bedrick, 1994, p. 53.
33. Crossley-Holland, *The Norse Myths*, p. 158.

Chapter Five: The Search for a Lost Sister

34. Quoted in John Sephton, trans., *The Saga of Erik the Red*, Icelandic Saga Database. https://sagadb.org.
35. Neil S. Price, *The Viking Way: Religion and War in Late Iron Age Scandinavia*. Oxford, UK: Oxbow, 2002, p. 64.
36. C. Keith Hansley, "The Myth of Nor and His Nor Way," Historian's Hut, July 26, 2019. https://thehistorianshut.com.

Chapter Six: Saga of the Legendary Ragnar

37. Quoted in Noah Tetzner, "Valhalla: How Viking Belief in a Glorious Afterlife Empowered Warriors," History, March 3, 2021. www.history.com.
38. Daniel Albert, "Eric Bloodaxe: The Story of the Royal Viking Warrior," Life in Norway, November 2, 2023. www.lifeinnorway.net.
39. Emma Groeneveld, "Ragnar Lothbrok," World History Encyclopedia, August 31, 2018. www.worldhistory.org.
40. Quoted in Northvegr Foundation, "The Tale of Ragnar's Sons: Part 1," trans. Peter Tunstall, 2005. https://jillian.rootaction.net.
41. Quoted in Northvegr Foundation, "The Tale of Ragnar's Sons: Part 2," trans. Peter Tunstall, 2005. https://jillian.rootaction.net.
42. Quoted in Tom Shippey, *Laughing Shall I Die: Lives and Deaths of the Great Vikings*. London: Reaktion, 2018, p. 87.
43. Luciano Anastasi, "Ragnar Lodbrok: The Viking Legend and His Epic Saga," Medieval History, June 7, 2023. https://historymedieval.com.

FOR FURTHER RESEARCH

Books

Jason Dodd, *Norse Mythology: A Collection of the Best Norse Myths*. West Sacramento, CA: Rivercat, 2024.

Gunnar Hylnsson, *Norse Myths, Paganism, Magic, Vikings, and Runes*. Self-published, 2022.

Dorling Kindersley, *Eyewitness: Viking*. New York: Dorling Kindersley, 2024.

Carolyne Larrington, *The Norse Myths That Shape the Way We Think*. London: Thames and Hudson, 2023.

Mathias Nordwig, *Norse Mythology for Kids*. Eagle, ID: Rockridge, 2020.

Henry Romano, *Myths and Legends of the Norse*. London: DTTY, 2022.

Internet Sources

Thomas Apel, "Loki," Mythopedia, December 8, 2022. https://mythopedia.com.

Lara Colrain, "Norse Pantheon: 10 Fascinating Gods and Goddesses," The Collector, October 21, 2023. www.thecollector.com.

Mike Greenberg, "Odin's Discovery of the Runes," Mythology Source, November 9, 2020. https://mythologysource.com.

Odin's Treasures, "Ragnar Lothbrok: Separating the Man from the Myth," 2024. https://odinstreasures.com.

Mark Oliver, "8 Norse Gods with Stories You'll Never Learn in School," All That's Interesting, December 15, 2021. https://allthatsinteresting.com.

Rhianna Padman, "Norse Cosmology: What Does the Universe Look like in Norse Mythology?," The Collector, July 2, 2023. www.thecollector.com.

Sons of the Vikings, "Viking Lore: A Quick Intro to Norse Eddas and Sagas," July 3, 2020. https://sonsofvikings.com.

Swedish History Museum, "Odin: The One-Eyed Father," Historiska. https://historiska.se.

Noah Tetzner, "Valhalla: How Viking Belief in a Glorious Afterlife Empowered Warriors," History, March 3, 2021. www.history.com.

Websites

A Beginner's Guide to Norse Mythology, Life in Norway
www.lifeinnorway.net/norse-mythology
Norway-based British translator and expert on the Viking age Jess Scott wrote this easy-to-read, nicely illustrated site, which contains dozens of links to topics relating to the Norse myths, including the main sources of the well-known Norse tales.

Hurstwic
www.hurstwic.com
Independent American scholar William R. Short, widely known as a leading expert on Norse culture, and especially Viking warfare, oversees this fact-filled website. It includes numerous links not only to the Norse myths but also to Viking daily life, ships, arms and armor, language, and much more.

Life in Norway
www.lifeinnorway.net/?s=mythology
This online guide to Norwegian life, culture, and history includes links to many articles about Norse mythology. The site includes articles about Eric Bloodaxe, the Jotnar, the gods and goddesses, and some of the many other creatures and beings found in Norse mythology.

Norse Mythology for Smart People
https://norse-mythology.org
Written by David McCoy, a noted scholar of Norse myths and folklore, this site contains a rounded, detailed look at the Norse myths, with numerous links to supportive articles, including ones on the various Norse gods, Norse cosmology, Viking culture, and diverse Norse writings.

World History Encyclopedia
www.worldhistory.org/Norse_Mythology
This website has a large selection of articles about Norse mythology. It includes links to information about Ragnar Lothbrok and other heroes, the mythological realms and creatures, the gods and goddesses, and many aspects of Norse life.

Note: Boldface page numbers indicate illustrations.

PICTURE CREDITS

Cover: AF Fotografie/Alamy Stock Photo

6: Maury Aaseng
10: © The Holbarn Archive/Bridgeman Images
13: Heritage Image Partnership Ltd/Alamy Stock Photo
14: Hatteviden/Shutterstock
18: Classic-Ads/Alamy Stock Photo
21: © Look and Learn/Bridgeman Images
25: © Look and Learn/Bridgeman Images
29: Fine Art Images/Newscom
32: Ivy Close Images/Alamy Stock Photo
35: © Look and Learn/Bridgeman Images
37: Ivy Close Images/Alamy Stock Photo
41: Ivy Close Images/Alamy Stock Photo
44: Ivy Close Images/Alamy Stock Photo
49: © DeA Picture Library/Bridgeman Images
50: Alamy Stock Photo
53: Alamy Stock Photo

ABOUT THE AUTHOR

Classical historian and award-winning author Don Nardo has written numerous acclaimed volumes about ancient civilizations and peoples. They include more than four dozen overviews of the mythologies of the Sumerians, Babylonians, Egyptians, Greeks, Romans, Persians, Celts, Chinese, Aztecs, Hindus, Native Americans, and others. Nardo, who also composes and arranges orchestral music, lives with his wife, Christine, in Massachusetts.